ASLEEP
INSIDE
MANIA

BY: NELSON MIRANDA

Copyright ©2015 By Nelson Miranda
All rights reserved. In accordance with
the U.S Copyright Act of 1976

ISBN-13:
978-0692507940

ISBN-10:
0692507949

For Zarryn and Kairi

My Love, My Hope

A special thanks

to my dear Watson

"THE CLINICAL"

Watch this wretched hand write

Hanging upon my requisite gimmick

Losing myself inside the lined graph

Allowing unwanted company to mimic

Call down upon me callus words

Drawn from an intense flame

While this transmission to ink

Mirrors remarks of the clinically insane

Know this as the reasoning

Botched ideas sinking towards the brink

They knew me all to well back then

The first time I was christened as Ink

Welcome to insanity

I will be your delighted host

"THE MUSEUM"

Color me as calligraphy

Precisely purposed strokes

Capture my fears with tainted ebony

Eliciting stills of aged ghosts

Be cognizant of my sorrow

The deeper the pages are stained

While my eyes willfully borrow

Moisture from the frigid rain

Appease my dwindling desire

Forged upon a defective foundation

The pilot has omitted the fire

Preventing my necessary re-creation

This completed rendition taunts

Veiled meaning in plain sight

The artistic shall ignore the haunt

Substituting day in place of night

"THE JURY"

Calculated misjudgments I have worn

Heavily through tattered imagery

Amazingly able to keep human pace

While lacking much needed energy

A swine lollygags around its fodder

Grotesque in its animalistic appearance

Who will sense its beating heart

Without judgments toward adherence

View me as you must

Ridicule with sharpened tongues

Scream with your loud silence

As sound waves reverberate my lungs

I am still a human being

A breathing, soulful vessel

So meet these glaring eyes with bravery

For my soul I keep safely nestled

"THE ESCAPE"

I remain a befuddled mess
A diagram of complex calculations
The taste of alcohol numbs sensibility
Tomorrow will lack needed meditation

My stomach churns sour
As I contemplate life's decisions
My eyes fix upon nothing at all
Lacking coordination with precision

I shatter through minor fractures
A knife-like sensation inside my rib cage
The aged demons begin to reappear
Their baritone screams filled with rage

Such a vicious, territorial cycle
I wish to escape such folly
A mere reflection of ideals
that shall prevent my calling

"THE WOLF"

Awakening under peaceful night
A rustling coat with sleepy eyes
Quietly gazing into the shadows
Beholding the glow of lit fireflies

Feeling the warmth of familiarity
Traversing through the grassy blades
These eyes were meant to divide souls
Slicing through the foggy haze

Lazily strolling fields of forgotten mines
It would seems man wishes his fellow to cease
Little ones frolic and play in these fields
Yet I am the one referred to as a beast

The nearby lake tastes of crystals
Upon this dehydrated tongue
This reflection awakens stifling desires
As a howl escapes energized lungs

Sounds of admirers are hushed
They judge by sharp teeth and bravery
So alone I journey with no equal
While subject to a different form of slavery

The moon leads me by the hand
Knowing its rival has rejected my sight
Transmitting sadness through a screaming glow
Her compassion soothes my plight

On the precipice of the highest point
The crescent is my listening ear
As my songs echo through the galaxy
My verses of hurt only elicit fear

"THE MARIONETTE"

Beginning the state of hypnosis

Inside the embattlement of a dream

Insecurities grabbing at the threads

While I unravel at withering seams

Decadence is a dangerous sin

The glutton's foolish game of chance

Grasping strands among the fingers

Perform the puppeteer's favorite dance

Adjusting to the ramblings of a cynic

As wood shavings fall down like rain

It is difficult to hold on to brittle strings

While learning the meaning of clinically insane

Have fun manipulating these arches

For I will soon learn how to escape

You will be lost and absent of your favorite toy

As the bringer delivers your fate.

"THE HILLSIDE"

Shadowed laterals capture stars
A bitter taste seeps inside the hinge
Tickling strands of diminishing strength
The closer realization upon a fringe

Attraction towards a needed rescue
Arms spread out as eagle's grace
If you peer inside my hazel eyes
Behold a soul not easily erased

Independence is learned through brimstone
Absent of this, though I have burned
Dark figures often walk beside me
Their quiet intentions hard to discern

True purpose is an endless journey
Edgings of a new horizon remain out of view
I carry a bouquet of crumbled lilies
Hoping that you will be there too

"THE AWAKENING"

I began my babbling story

Upon her ivory skin

This living breathing canvas

Absorbs happiness and sin

An undesirable punitive hand

Was unmatched by her candor

My eyes were transfixed

Upon her smile of splendor

As the burning red took over

Inner demons began to fly

Panting heavily this escaped convict

Wishing for the chance to say goodbye

Yet she responded with grace

Disregarding my mental behavior

I do well at playing the martyr

Though this time another played savior

Now with this pen I stand taught

Lessons never before learned

They lost all control over me

As the strings of the marionette burned

Singed hair flowed from above

The specimen of awakening breath

She pierced her fiery eyes into my heart

As the shadows flew to escape their death

"THE MOMENT"

Simplistic realms of fostered ideas
Testing insignificant resolution
Amazing how scars of purpose
Could save a mind from dissolution

My prayers are internalized
A temple filled with echoed screams
Haunted by dry cackling bones
The director's cut of seismic dreams

There beyond the edges of distinction
I beheld an answer wrapped in song
For once in my menial life
The distance had not felt as long

Attainable finally has true meaning
Viewed no longer as a detestable word
The line was hazy if not indistinguishable
The separation of reality from the absurd

In the middle remained the idea

As peaceful as waves kissing a dock

A dream realized lived on a watered field

Happily feeding sheep missing their flock

The dew drops stuck upon its nose

Making the thought alive through physicality

I now know your existence is factual

It is my duty to make you my reality

"THE SAMURAI"

Bind my solidarity inside thick webs
Craftily catching wicked intentions
Though I shall remain absolute
Belittling your evil deception

I am numb inside the distance
Ready to defend my requests
As your mind is full of darkness
Knowing little of what is best

Seconds seep past imperfections
The acidic properties of time
Picking up the blade as a virgin child
Ready to take back what is mine

Obstacles test a warrior's resolve
While the arrogant prey on the weak
Silence will be the pattern arranged
With bloodshot eyes you will hear me speak

Upon the wings of a glorious phoenix
The flames fuse together tattered skin
Filled with a new found vigor
Melding glory over an abundance of sin

Breaking deep into the encampment
Crashing down from the skies above
This forged steel shall taste victory
Emptying my heart of misguided love

"THE INSOMNIAC"

The screaming realization of silence
Bends through yearning canals and drums
Sunlight breaks the drawn curtains
If only to search for the aquatic hum

These sheets neglect my never ending chill
For they were never meant for bone
Longing fingers may search for skin
Realizing only that you lie alone

Every muscle used in order to stand
Leaving nothing left to produce a smile
Pace is the trick, as pacing is my disorder
With thoughts as deep as the blue Nile

The staircase is a spiraling abyss
Though I am no stranger to the void
Let my beaten eyes meet those of the one
Filing darkness under a mere choice

Lungs often forget the pattern of breathing
Unless met with thick pungent smoke
My mind should be brimming inside memories
Though I cannot recall a single note

I stumble through the cavern's depths
As the worn flint struggles to create fire
Setting aside my dreams and wishes
I shall remain a shoulder for hire

" THE SILENT "

The universe collects the Galaxies together
Watching over them at a loving pace
Constellations cover the great expanse
While meteors fall downward with haste

The milky planets dance in perfect unison
With a bright star lighting their way
Earth in her grandeur quietly spins
Truly beautiful beneath the gray

The sky holds clouds without effort
While they themselves hold the very rains
A blanket of sand covers the great deserts
With mountains overshadowing grassy plains

Inside the bustling city nights
An array of happenings commence
Neon lights brighten the dark sky
As shadows hide behind their pretense

Neath this simple rooftop

Covered by frail sheets

I am lost inside emotion

Feeling utterly incomplete

Though I am merely a speck of nothingness

These lips speak wishes when I'm alone

The universe groans in silence

As I beg for a place to call home

"THE LIE"

Watching the Dame with anticipation

As she floats atop the whiskey waves

Teasing me with her sensual moves

While I beg for a small sweet taste

You are the one that understands

As you numb away the dreadful pain

My life has been a torrential downpour

With a sip you protect me from the rain

Inside this lie I am slowly dying

While two little ones learn their new life

I was never meant to walk freely

On hands and knees I reach my height

The warm room feels hazy

These eyes wallow in sorrow

So many will beg for sunrise

As I look to disappear into the hollow

Yes, this is selfishness manifested

I have silently waited my turn

Judgment quickly reaches narrow lips

Though I dare you to justify my burns

Nature looks to correct the enigma

As vicious faces gnash their teeth

I have become a silent martyr

Singing the tired ones off to sleep

My lullaby never came to existence

My song is a shovel against the dirt

The beautiful ones fill my head with lies

For I have been shown my true worth

The mound is readied and freshly stirred

As the gravedigger wipes his brow

Tomorrow is a pipe dream

Reality is the here and now

"THE CAVE"

Collateral damage with sad eyes shut
Deemed necessary through the requisite
Sound waves will travel slower than time
The opportunity for you to voice your sentiment

While ink flows quietly, will I win your hearts
As haze rises from the gun powder's smoke
Will the letters inscribed in front of my eyes
Become an erroneous sense of ones hope

My heart implodes violently at the thought
Your seeing my shadow devoid of detail
This strength should not have evaporated
With seemingly no excuse for me to fail

Inclement weather saturates these bones
With hollowed cheeks cold and damp
I found the source of shattered glass
The trail led to a dimly fired lamp

"THE BEAUTIFUL"

He arrived in a furtive manner

As he took you within sleep

I should have been at your side

Collecting memories I could safely keep

The day was as a bad dream

A realization of consequences

I took advantage of your multiple victories

Only to be introduced to reality's harsh impressions

I am deeply sorry for my absence

Now my memories of you are swayed

You shall remain a permanent fixture

Of this complex beating heart, always

I shall not be there to greet you

As you slowly open newfound eyes

Though two precious angels will be waiting

And I know you will enjoy the surprise

"THE JOURNEY"

I continue through mass hysteria
The dripping caverns of my mind
Making sense of the ledges and traps
Realizing fear plagues all of mankind

One foot in front of the next
A slurred trail left behind in the mud
Life has been tumultuous path
Still I continue through the tears and blood

A rock mass stood before me
Ancient braille carved upon its face
The dialect was foreign to the demons
Its words kept my feet at their pace

This astoundingly simple message
Appeared before my eyes as a memory
My heart filled with exultation
As I was circled by the curious enemy

"You can have your wishes and desires
You can escape doubt's burning fires
Impedance and action, separated by a thin wire
You have the ability to prove them all liars"

The shadowy creatures made their retreat
As my aura pierced their crooked sight
Tomorrow holds an array of possibilities
And I have yet to reach my complete height

" THE TIME MACHINE "

Created inside a lightning storm
Lungs filled with bated breath
Whispering a transcript of secrets
With words the mind easily forgets

Traveling back through the gates of time
Away from a life that is bereaved
I beheld the dying tree in its youth
Watching the birth of sprouted leaves

It was a freshly grown seedling
Ready to begin a journey new
With no inkling of the shadows that await
Knowing only of the peaceful blue

I watered my dreams with a single tear
To give my future the mechanism to cope
Seeing my ideals inside their virgin state
Filled my heart with a glimmer of hope

I contemplated moving the seed to soil

To help my fragile state along

I let myself continue on the rocky gravel

For roots need tribulation to grow strong

Returning to the rotting old tree

Tracing fingers across the brittle bark

Dumbfounded at the sight before me

In four letters, the teardrop left its marked

-Hope-

"THE HIGHWAY"

That peaceful feeling of nature

Sound waves touching my subconsciousness

Lulled by the splatters upon the laminated glass

As neon lights glow in the morning mist

The moon and sun still chasing tails

Dancing spectacles that lace their housing

The city sleeps inside damp streets

With lighted billboards silently touting

In this moment of forward direction

I find my way through my treacherous past

Just as the busy highways have moments of peace

I look for a handful that were built to last

I search for my own lyrical song

Comprised of a melodious victory speech

As a student of purposed viability

The road shall lead me to all I seek

"THE ILLUSIVE"

My adornment is of worn out pages
Molded from droplets even in drought
This world is filled with endless wonder
Bypassing the valve at the end of the spout

Wrinkled paper and smudged words
They stick together as close knit friends
Some peel away for a chance at content
Scanning the page until the periods end

Though I often find myself illegible
As disgust rages from the readers eyes
Quickly I am tossed away from sight
They wash their hands of a proper goodbye

I often question whether I am fictional
A complicated character in a boring play
While the audience shuffles through the exits
I am forced to hold all emotions at bay

"THE TRUTH"

Contrary to the maliciousness of others
Words with an edge capable of carving stone
While these quickly forget their senselessness
You are left naught but skin and bones

Contrary to your own personal beliefs
Feelings of being a valueless token
With each quake-driven step placed
You feel splinters turning limbs broken

Contrary to the life you may be experiencing
One filled with contention and strife
While you struggle with burning questions
Wondering why you deserve to breathe in life

Contrary to the heartache experienced
Battle scars bursting inside each stitch
Sinking knees buried in the mire
Where desperate leeches bleed for a kiss

Contrary to all of these and so much more
I shall love you proud and truly
While you dance inside the roaring fire
The shadows I see contain untold beauty

While your body wears battered signatures
I shall peacefully initial my place
Beyond the thorns there is a rose
Beyond sorrow lies your grace

"THE SURGEON"

Learning adaptability in the face of trial
Surely vital toward keeping one's sanity
Within the parchment of my yearning heart
I attempt to release all sorrow and vanity

Yet the negative attributes remain
Obstructing the flow of precious ink
Until it burrows deep into my being
Causing this flesh to rot and stink

I search frantically for the scalpel
With an aching desire to be rid of infection
The scar tissue is a strong deterrent
While wounds target my frail complexion

You are beholding a masterpiece
An enigma inside bone and sinew
My eyes have become weighted with time
Seeing the darkness as few do

I have seen the demons dance and play
With sapped strength I offer little resistance
Contentment seems a mere dream
As I wallow in the tombs of my existence

Time is still while I live as an option
Having been fitted for my noose
They would gladly activate the trapdoor
If only I would let their imagination loose

"THE MATHMATICIAN"

A tenth of me is determination

Fighting against fierce opposition

The heart lives on lust and desire

While the mind carries its own rendition

A tenth of me is horribly frightened

As the claws of monsters reverberate

Their eyes glare in a hungered passion

Primed to destroy if only I hesitate

A tenth of me is selflessness

Writing for those that beg for a voice

You are beautiful and deeply loved

Despite the lies, you do have a choice

A tenth of me is pessimistic

With a lack of water for musty eyes

Where you see hello as just the beginning

I see it as an inevitable goodbye

A tenth of me is utterly broken
Trenching through devoid marshlands
The hourglass splintered against time
As palm races to catch dwindling sand

These puzzle pieces make up my soul
Though I am lacking what is true
I would be whole and complete
If my other half was you

"THE WHISPERER"

I found her amidst the echoing silence
Notwithstanding the rasp of bated breath
Having worn a pretty cloak of euphoria
Covering transparent skin hinting of death

Wolves circled with muddied paws
Awaiting the word to end her sorrow
Opening her mouth she sang so beautifully
With lyrics absent of a foretold tomorrow

Her resonating voice awakened sleeping ears
As she conquered their restless souls
Reduced to pups that begged for their mother
Sharp claw and fang seemed no longer bold

I approached in awe of her candor
As she stood somber inside the night
Her eyes hesitated to meet mine
Guarded as though weary of my sight

Her presence made me feel at home
Feeling warm in the aura of her embrace
Wishing to drink from the spring of life
Without the disgust of its bitter taste

She had always been seen in color
Her smile forced to project light
She only wanted an accepting soul
Willing to see her in black and white

"THE WISH"

The wretched pain in my hollow heart

Matched the hesitation of forward progress

Though with valiant efforts I fought

My yearning allowed for little success

Running lead to a pitiful crawl

Until I was paralyzed and left still

It is impossible to appreciate the beautiful view

With eyes unable to see over the window sill

Filled with undeniable fault

In secret I battle through daunting pain

Know I would give the skin off my bones

Just to protect you from the rain

Key moments of life's passing joy

Have found me muddy and unkempt

Only seeing the grandeur of the world

Through hearts still too pure to resent

I cannot ask for understanding
An apology without anticipation of forgiveness
You are the very breath inside these tired lungs
Lacking your presence would render me loveless

"THE SHEPARD"

Grant me solitude in your bosom
As I approach your ankles dreadfully
These injuries are lacking approval
After wandering into the trap senselessly

Though you know my state of being
I, the gravel below the dust formation
Brought up through the fires of pain
These nerve endings have lost all sensation

Thus I became a ritualistic martyr
While the Lost one called me by name
I abandoned my promise of servitude
Becoming another tick toward his fame

Now on collapsed knees I am questioning
The worth of a disease-ridden sheep
Pondering over a timeless sacrifice
Awaiting seasons of eternal sleep

Would I be accepted back

Into your loving embrace?

Would you allow your warmth

To once again cover my disgrace?

" THE TREASURED "

A dance around my heart while wearing smiles

Skipping about with laughter and frivolity

Unaware that my center is comprised of you

And with two first breaths you changed my psychology

Your smiles have altered my very foundation

Filling the holes with undeserved love

When the sky cries tears of fiery rain

I know my wishes were received from above

When I held each one of you I was taught a lesson

Of dreams and happiness coming to fruition

I wish with everything I have to gain your approval

In this lifetime I have no greater mission

Though it may seem that I lurk in the shadows

My future lives and breathes with two angels in mind

Edge, please take care and protect my love

Bella, teach him how to be patient and kind

Support each other on the hazardous roads
Close your ears to murmurs and petty talk
Lift your eyes towards the promising sunrise
While I silently watch over you like a hawk

Pull apart the layers of this puzzling life
Until you reach the center of it all
My brave warriors, if you ever chose to fight
I would give my life before you would ever fall

"I used to believe that blank pages at the end of books were meant for the reader - as if the author was offering them the chance to rewrite the ending."

- Krista Lee

Dear reader,

    I thank you for taking this journey with me and diving in to the most personal places of my being. Whether you are a seasoned writer yourself or someone that enjoys reading poetry, I hope something in this book has resonated with you. The only thing left is the ending. I want you to decide that and write the finale for me. I would love your words to be a part of this experience as well. Please feel free to share the next page with me. I would love to see what your beautiful mind comes up with.

With love,

Nelson M

"

"

www.ingramcontent.com/pod-product-compliance
Lightning Source LLC
Chambersburg PA
CBHW061346040426
42444CB00011B/3111